Happy Tails,

Merlin

Razz

Claudia   Bruce

The Tail of Two Corgis

by Merlin and Razz
with Claudia and Bruce Winkle

Illustrated by
Penny Hauffe

This book is in memory of

Dobbie Bassett

the dedicated Cardigan
Welsh Corgi breeder
who brought us into
our Mom and Dad's lives.

Printed in USA   Published by: Merrazz-LLC   First Edition 2012

US $14.95   All rights reserved   ISBN# 1-978-0-9846868-0-3

CPSIA Compliance Information: Batch # 0112

For further CPSIA information contact RJ Communications, NY, NY, 800-621-2556.

 # This book belongs to:

_____

Hi!

My name is Merlin.

Just like Merlin the Magician.

Book of Spells

Eye of Toad

WING of BAT

Hi! My name is Razzamatazz.

You can call me Razz. Everyone does!

RAZZAMATAZZ

We are
Cardigan Welsh Corgi dogs.

We're Merlin and Razz,
the Corgis with the Tail...

We are brothers that almost look like twins.

One of the ways you can tell us apart is by the different markings on our funny faces.

Or, you can just look at our name tags.

As Cardigan Welsh Corgis, we were bred to herd animals like

cows,

sheep,

and even ducks...

But we don't have any of these at our house.

Soooo!

We herd our Mom

when she is wearing

her **BIG**, *funny*, *furry*, *and fuzzy slippers.*

Most of the time, we are very mischievous.
We like to pull up the rugs in the family room.

We pile them

into a

BIG heap.

(But only when Mom and Dad are not looking!)

We also like to clown around

and are famous for making you laugh out loud!

We like to go for *long* walks through our neighborhood and love to greet everyone we meet.

We make everyone *smile!*

When we get back from our walks, we are still full of energy and like to chase each other

around and around and around the couch.

It is one of our favorite games.

Try to catch us if you can!

As Cardigan Welsh Corgis,
we are also very intelligent.
We have our own special way of communicating.

After we eat,
if we are still
hungry,
we just turn over
our empty bowl
so Mom or Dad
can refill it.

PLEASE!

When we are thirsty and our water bowl is dry,
we pick it up and carry it around.
Usually the

CLANG,

CLANG,

CLANG

of the bowl

gets us some attention.

THANK YOU!

We are very loyal to our Mom and Dad.

We love to settle at their feet
and sometimes...
we all get to snuggle on the couch.

We are affectionate
and give hugs

and silly, sloppy kisses.

At the end of the day,
we gather all our
stuffed toys
into our beds
and fall asleep.

I am an AKC registered Cardigan Welsh Corgi.
Officially my name is "Dobcarr's The Magician".
My friends call me Merlin.

My first best friend, Jewel, called me Merman.
She was so funny and when she called me that
I would just crack up.

As you can probably guess, I have brought
magic and even some mischief in to my Mom
and Dad's lives.

I was born on March 7, 2009.
That makes my Sun sign Pisces.
I love taking long walks along the beach, and
since I have a double coat of fur, I prefer
low humidity.

I am the muse of our family.

I am also an AKC registered Cardigan Welch Corgi.
My official name is "Dobcarr's Razzamatazz".
As you know, everyone calls me Razz.

I chose my Mom and Dad by giving them lots of
puppy kisses on their faces.
I was just 4 weeks old when they held me
for the first time.

I was born on October 19, 2010.
That makes my Sun sign Libra.
I am pretty easy going and I love to read the
news on my iPad, preferably on my Mom's lap.

When Mom is home she helps me practice my tricks.

Besides eating hamburger, my favorite thing to do
is to be picked up and hugged by my Mom and Dad.

Be sure to visit our web site for more information about us.
www.Merrazz-LLC.com

Claudia, our Mom, is a Cardi (Cardigan Welsh Corgi) Mom and an Aussie (Australian Shepherd) Mom. Our Aussie brother is named Bear. Mom works for a large retail store chain. She travels a lot, and we miss her when she is on the road. She inspired us to write this book.

Bruce, our Dad, is an energy healer and teacher. Dad TRIES to take good care of us while Mom is out of town (read between the lines). Yet, Dad did take care of all the details for the publishing of this book.

Penny, our cute artist friend, smells like wet paint and greyhound dogs. She helped us tell our tail through her colorful illustrations.
Penny is a celebrated painter and sculptor. She created our oil portraits when we each turned one.
Please check her out at www.pennypaint.com

A special thanks to: Peny Lang for her editing review, Laura Lacroix-Johnson for her magical photos, Kathi Watts for our wonderful web site, Phil Whitmarsh for his expertise on printing, Patty Best and Cheri Dion for their marketing guidance.